This book belongs to:

____

____

Learning while having fun with...

Identifying the shapes

Writing each number

Knowing your colors

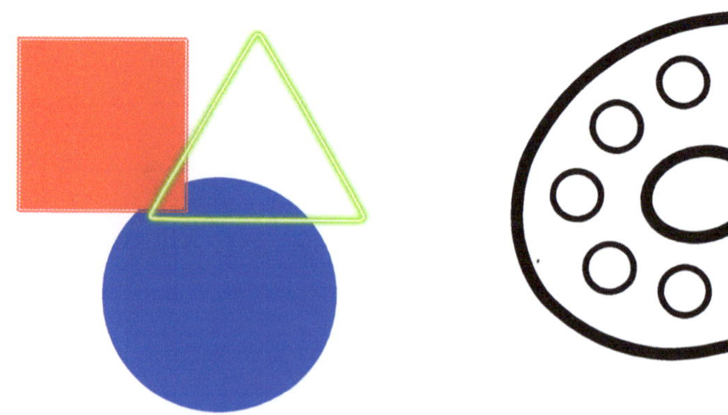

Shapes

____

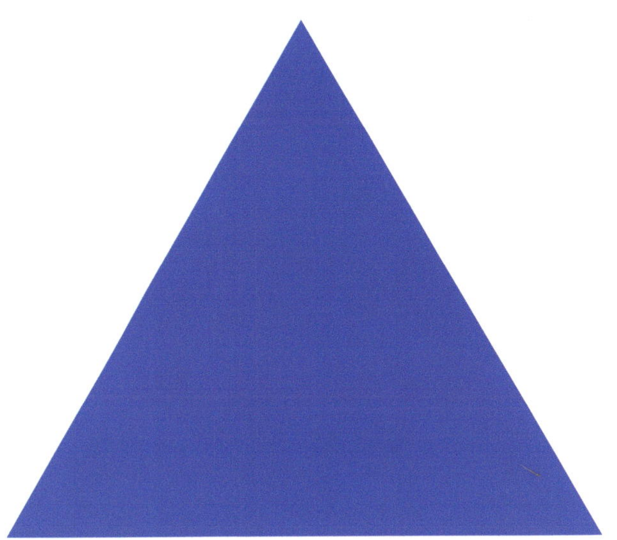

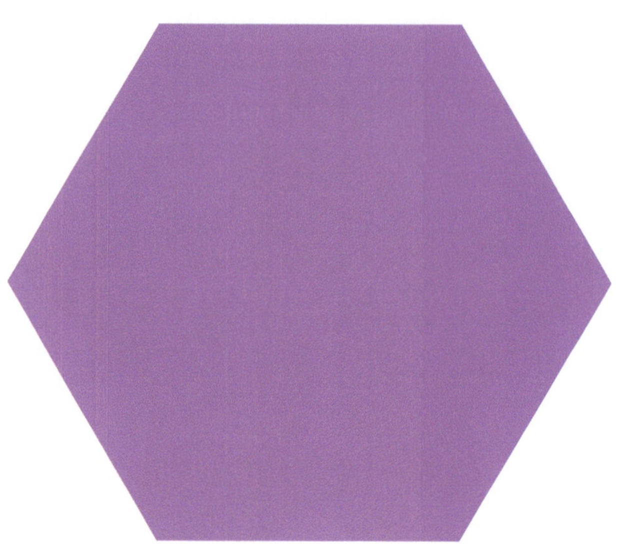

Numbers

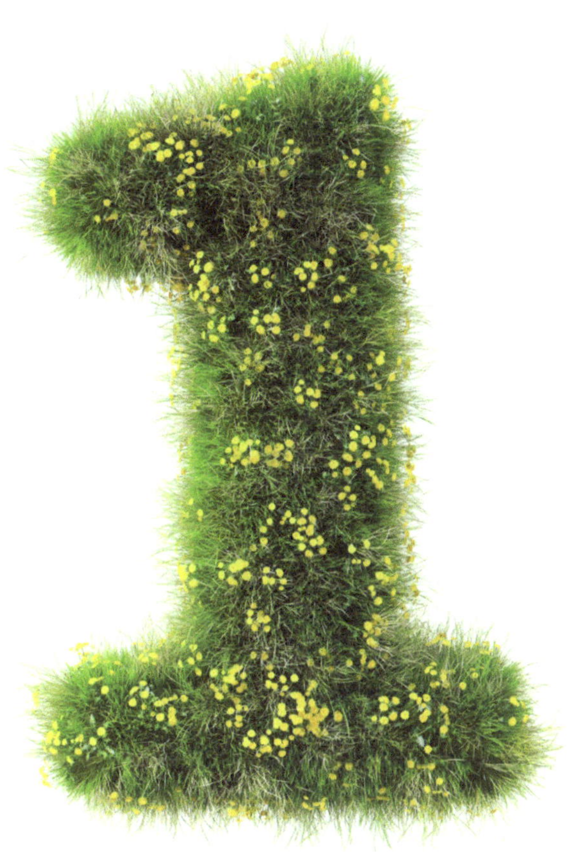

____

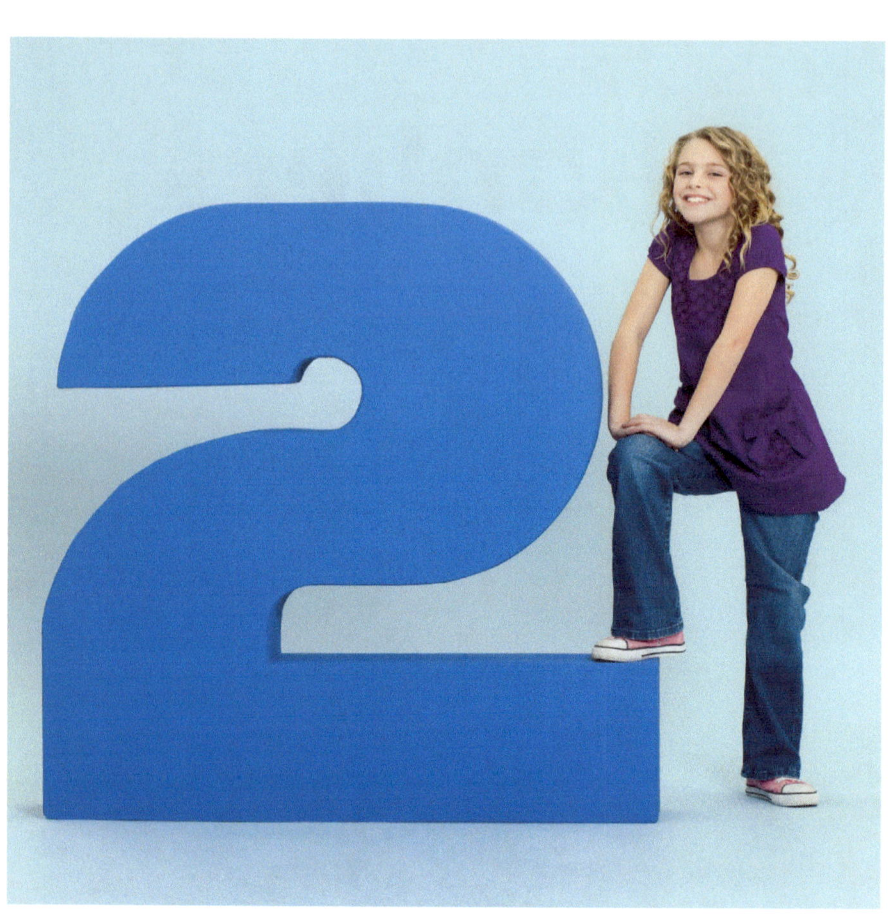

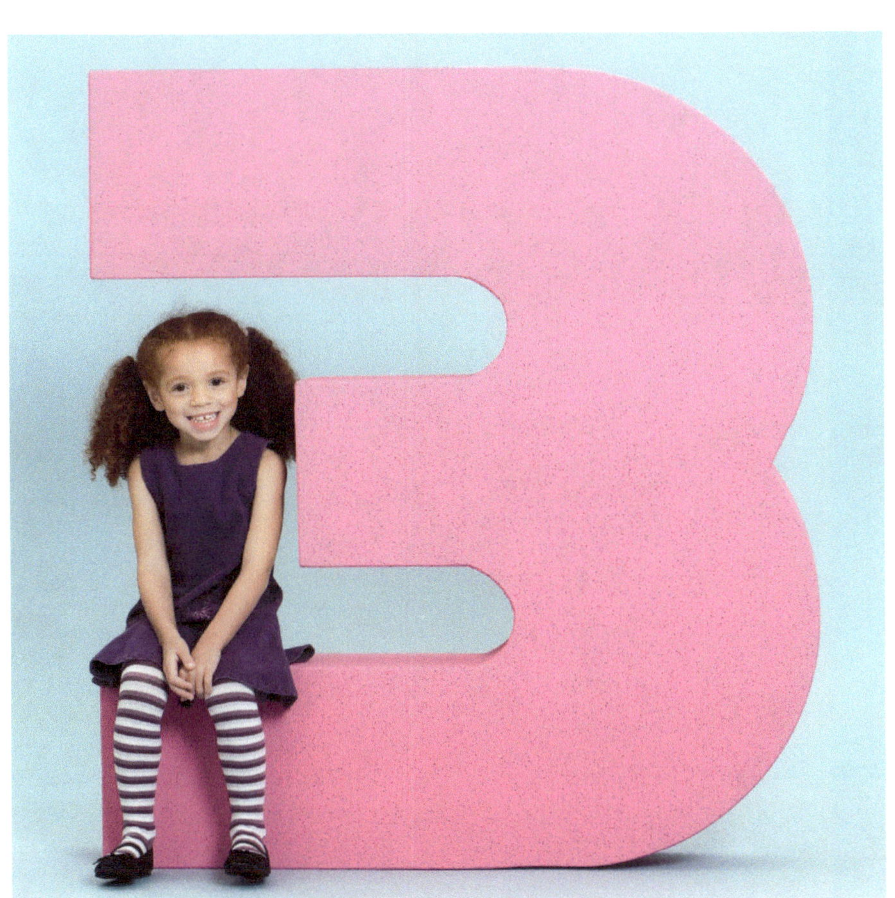

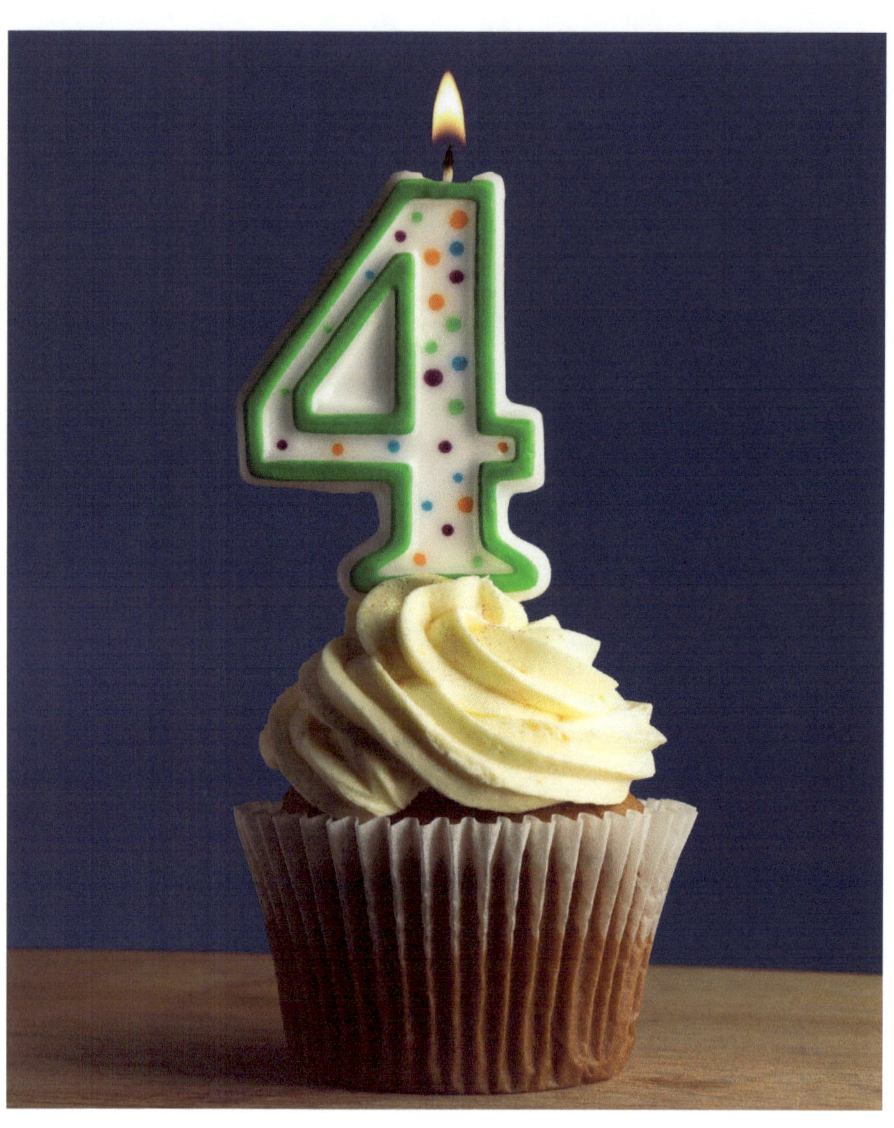

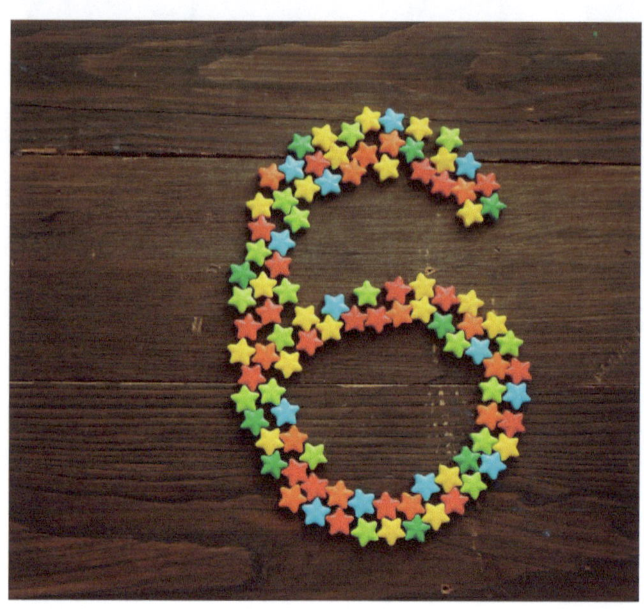

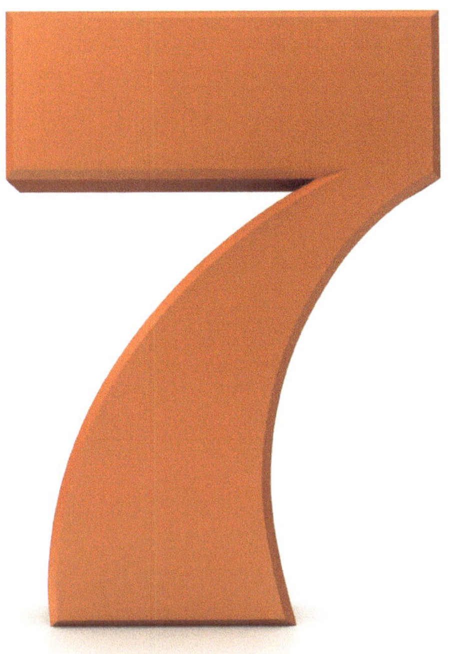

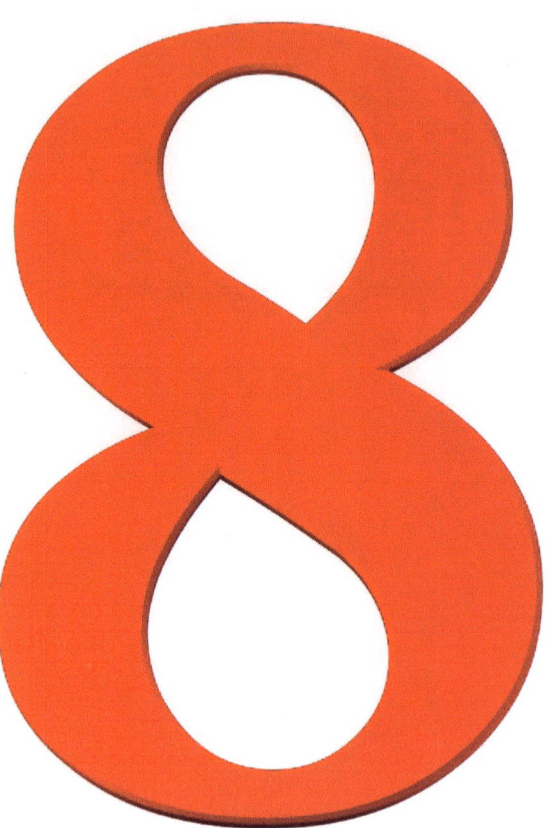

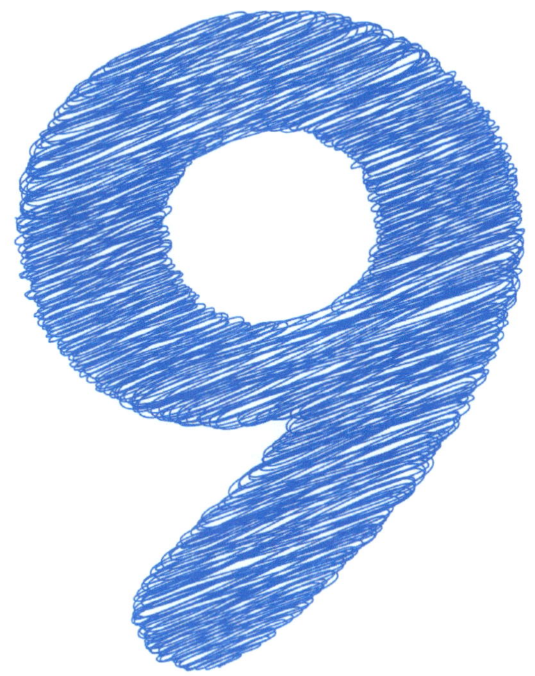

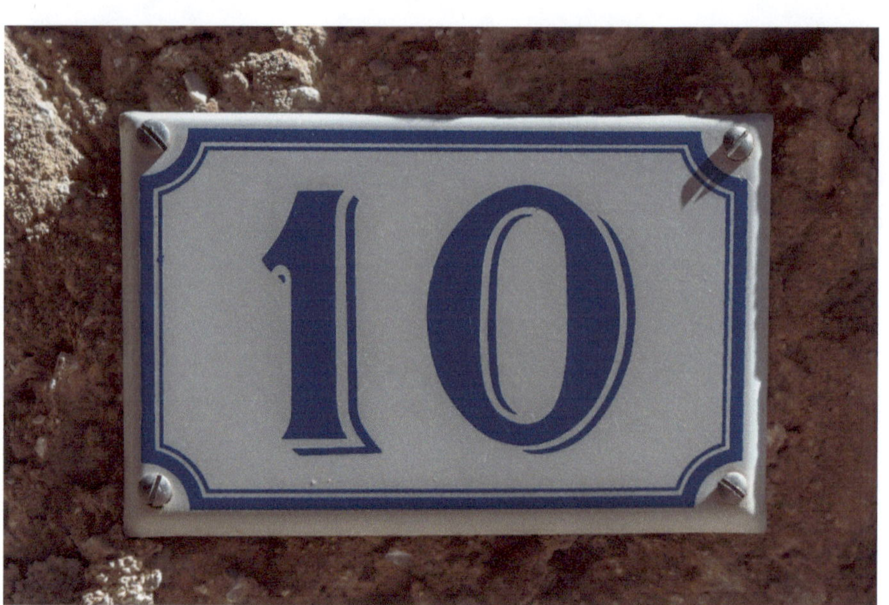

10

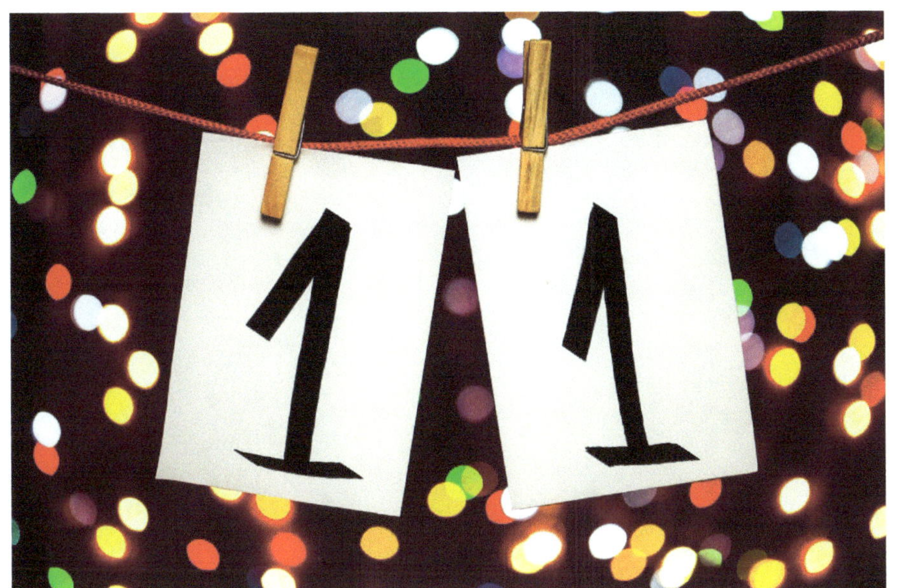

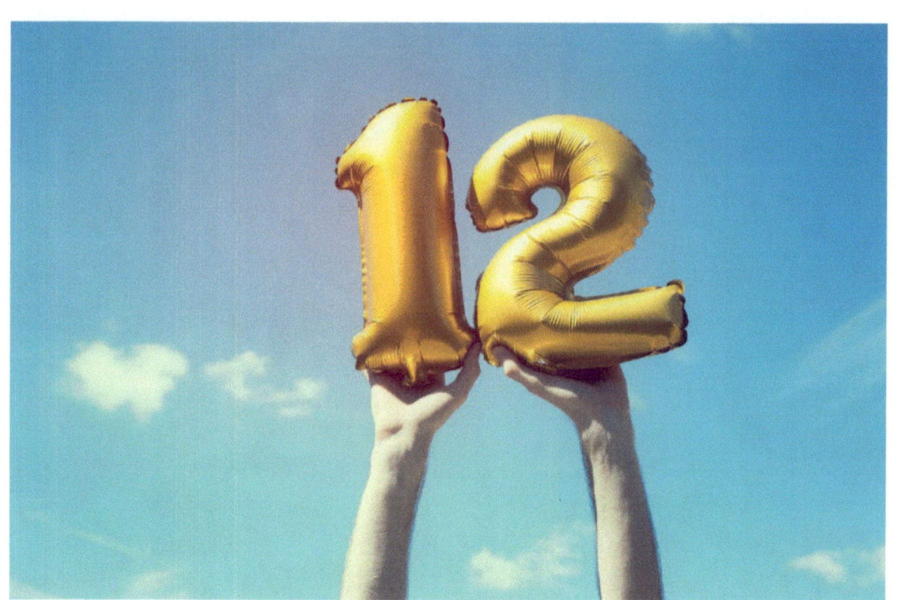

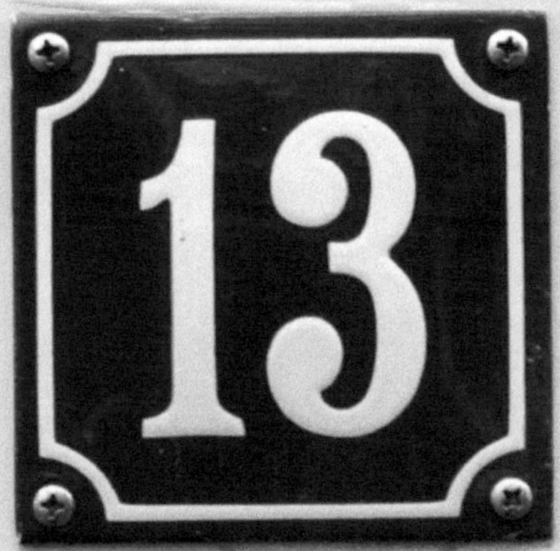
13

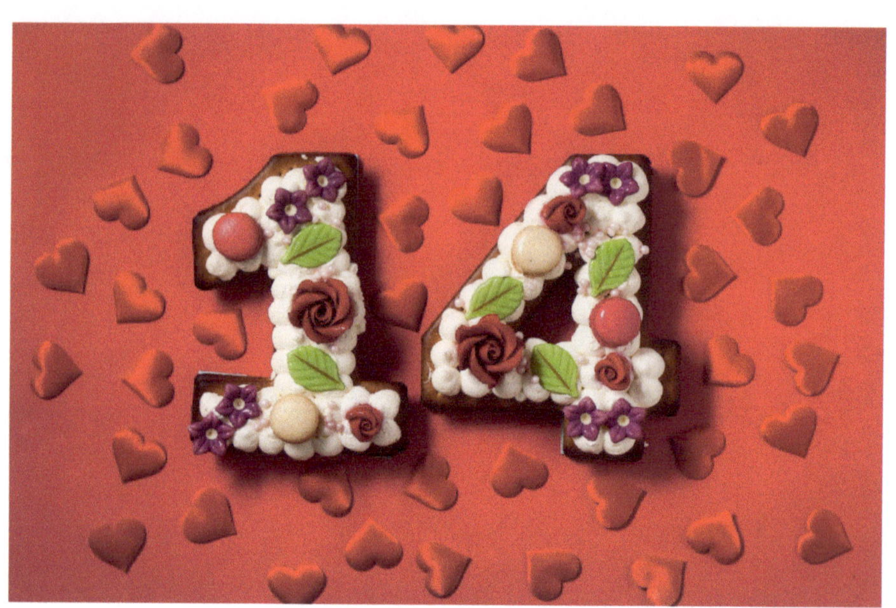

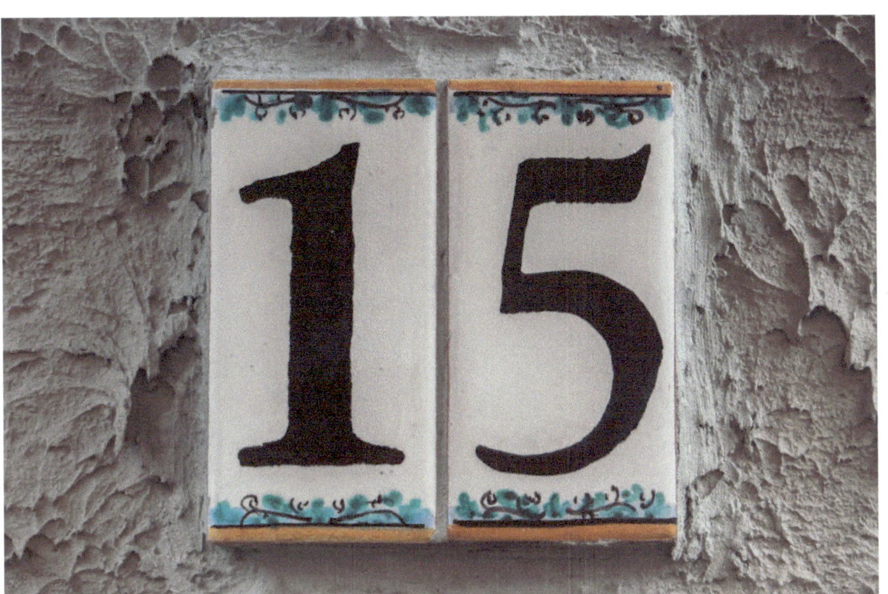

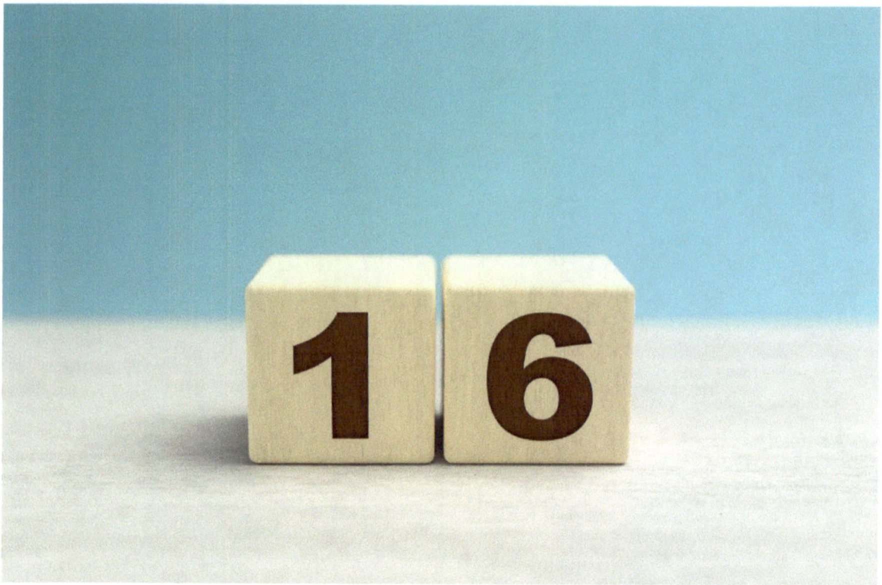

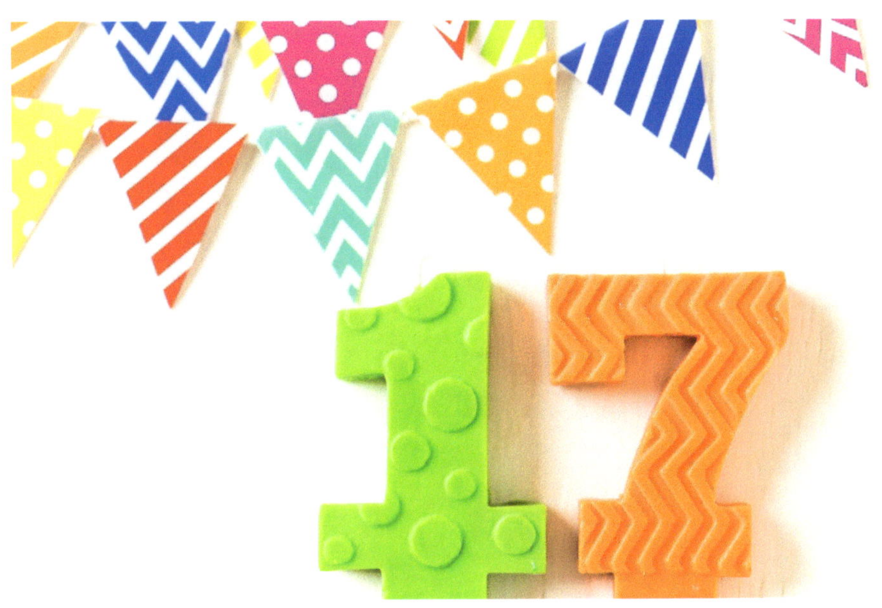

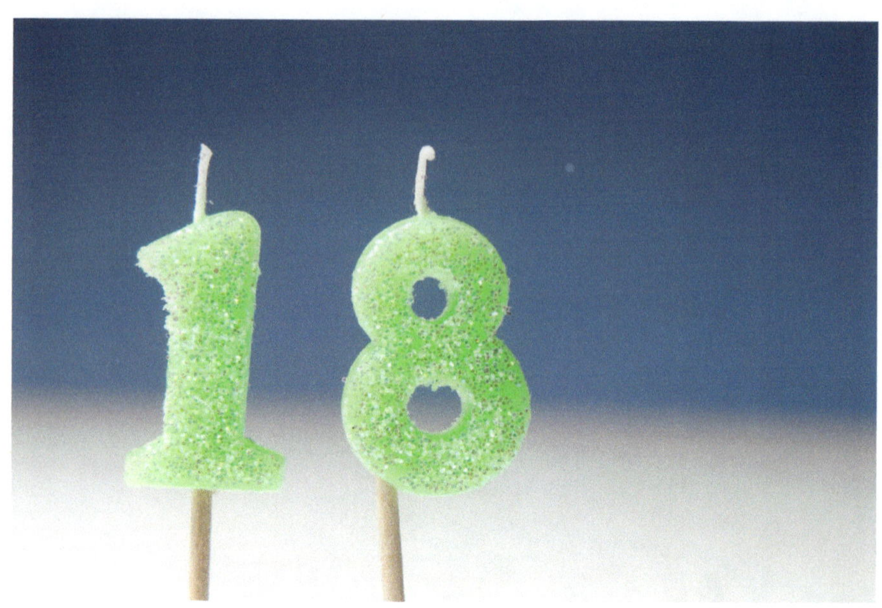

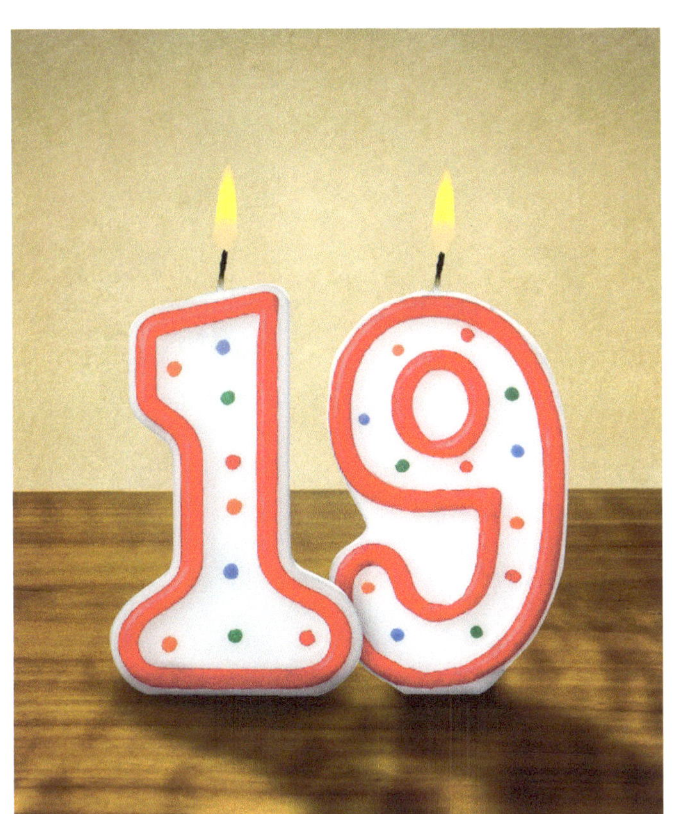

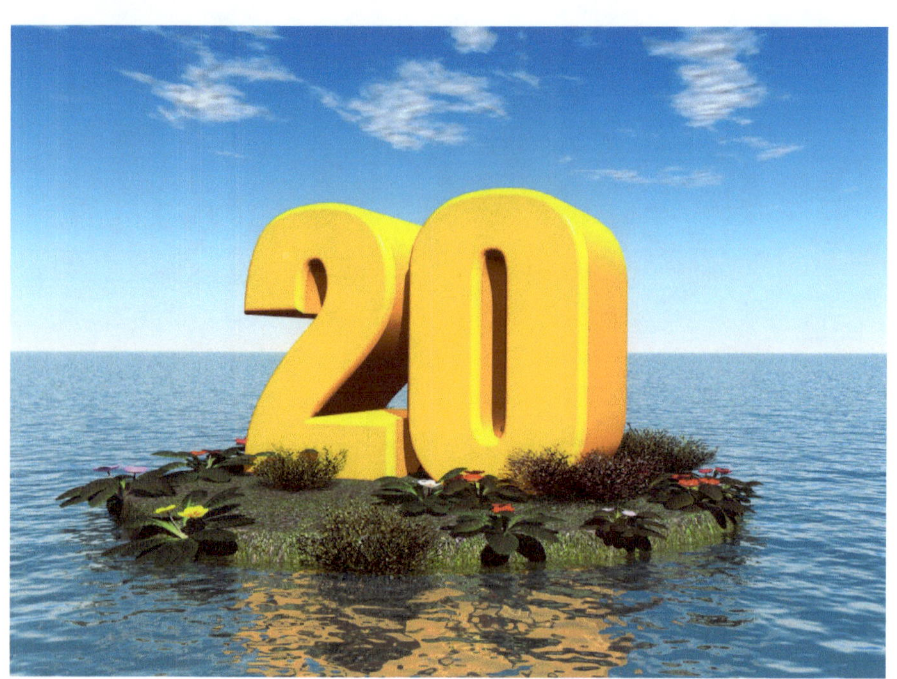

Colors

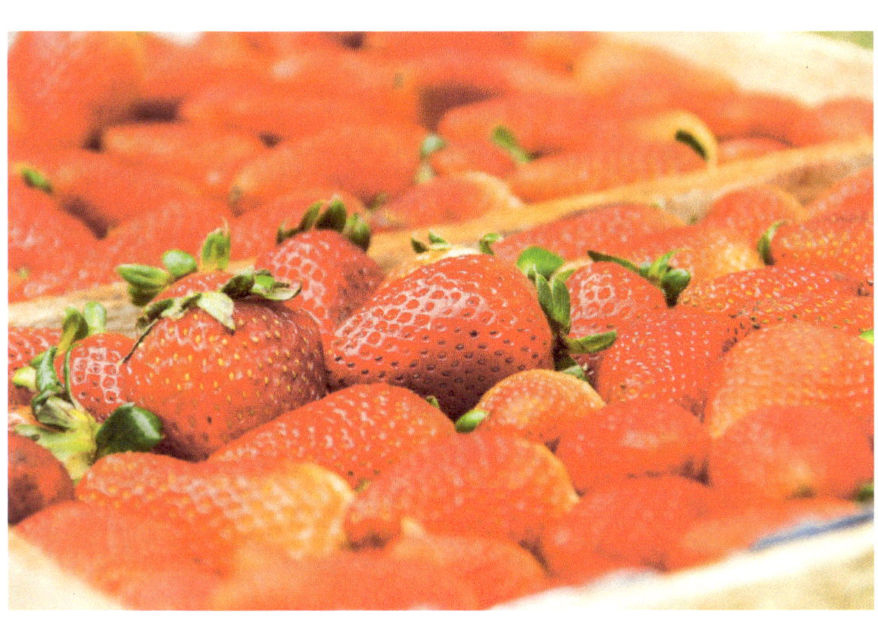

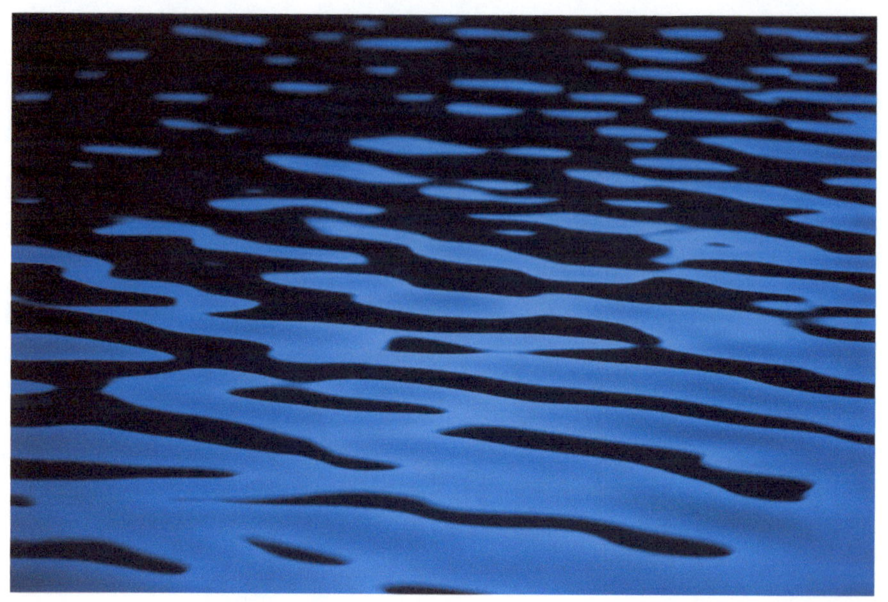

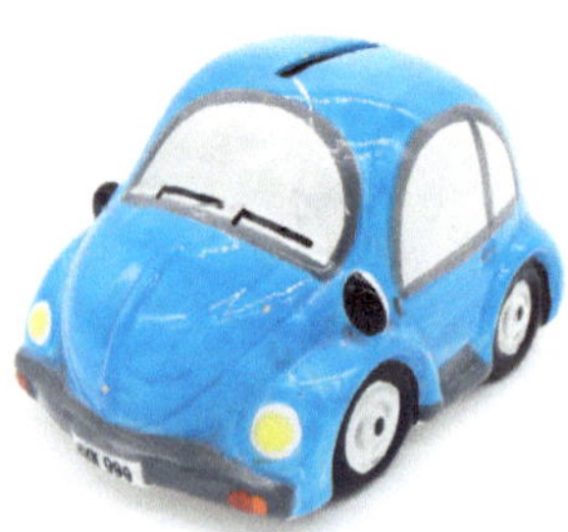 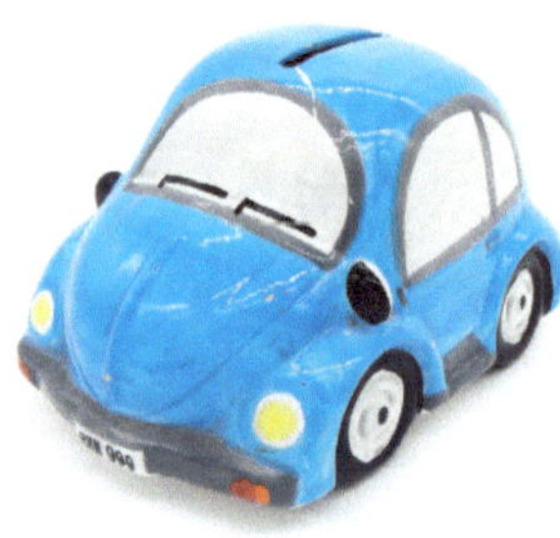

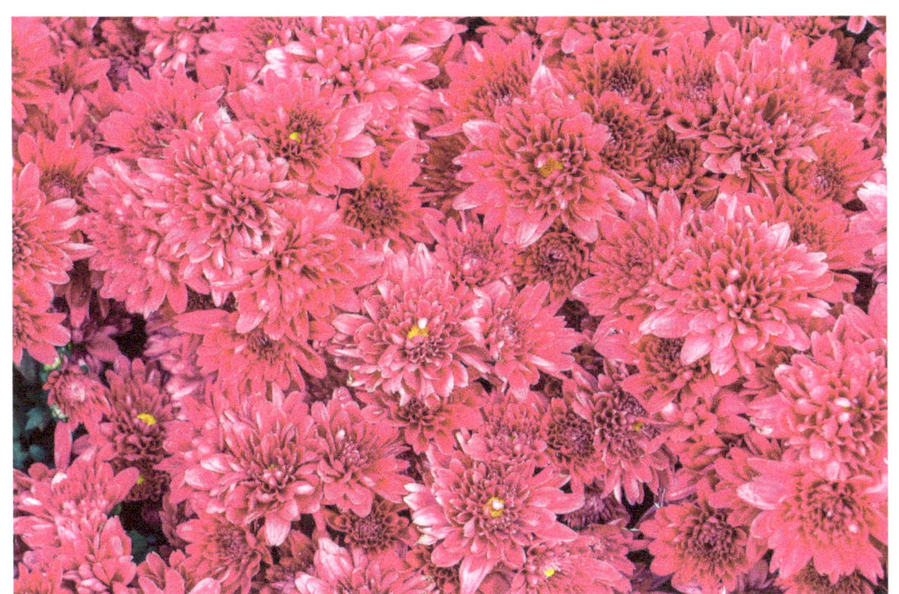

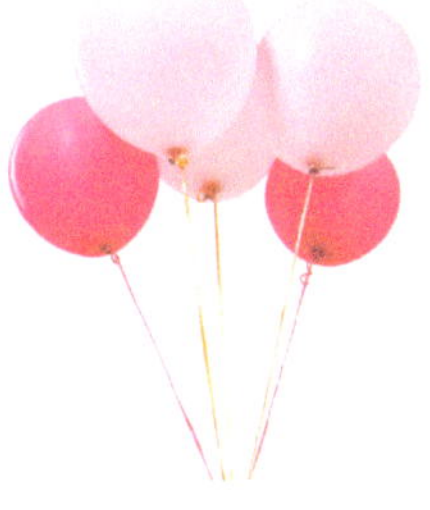

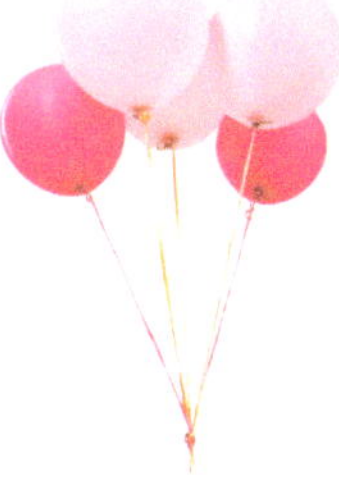

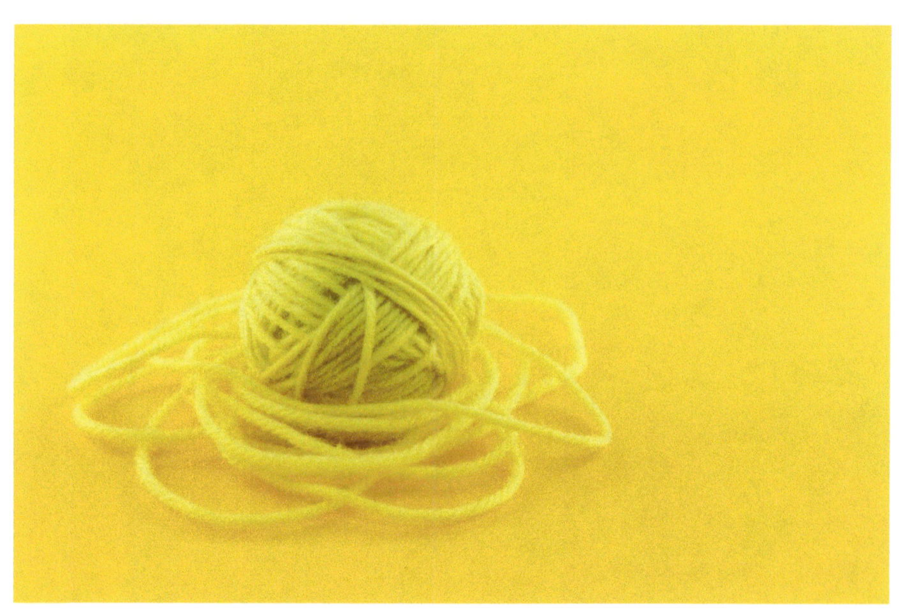

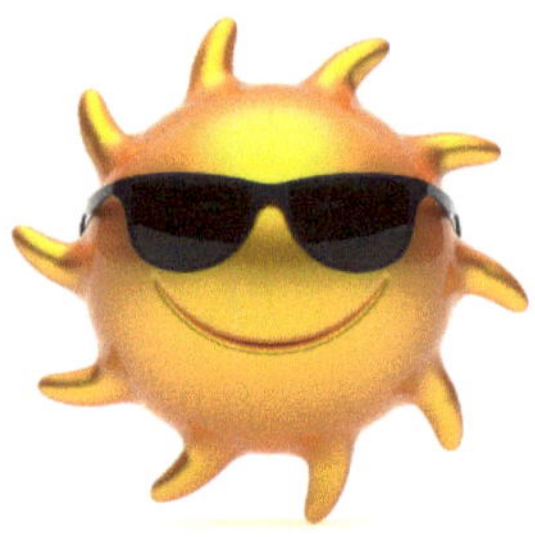

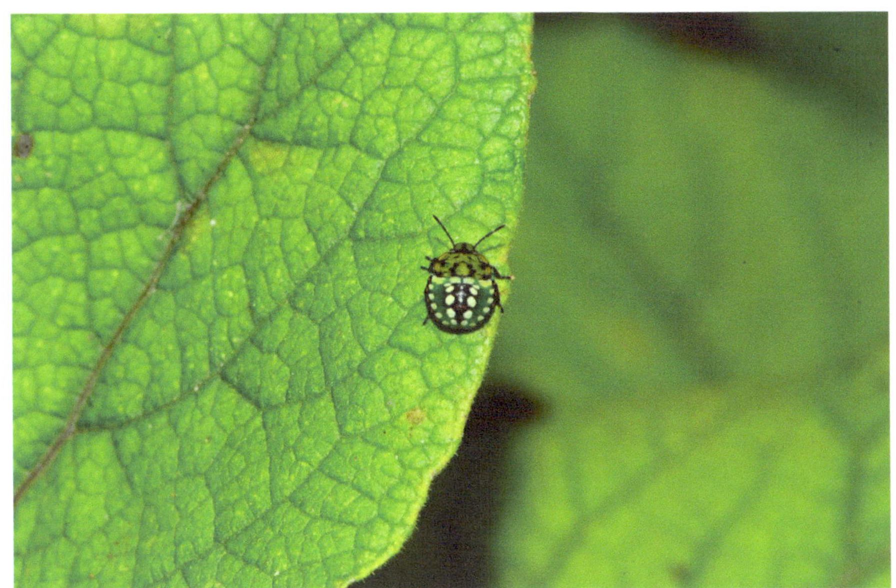

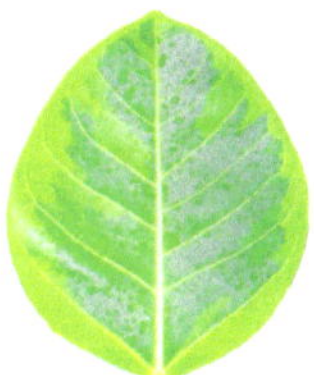 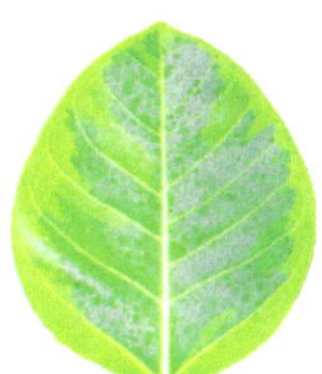 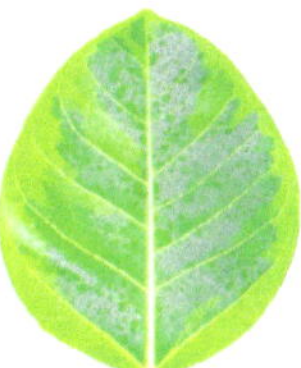

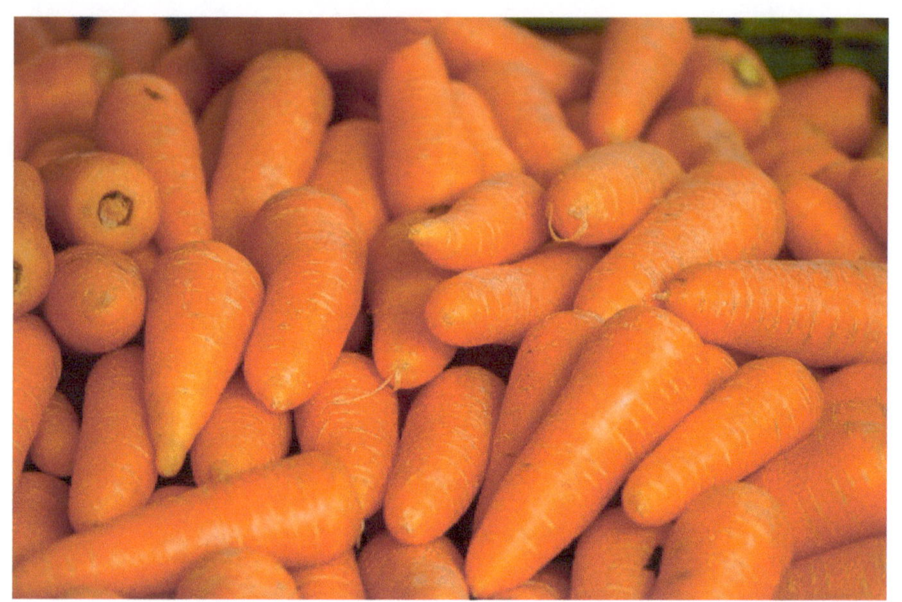

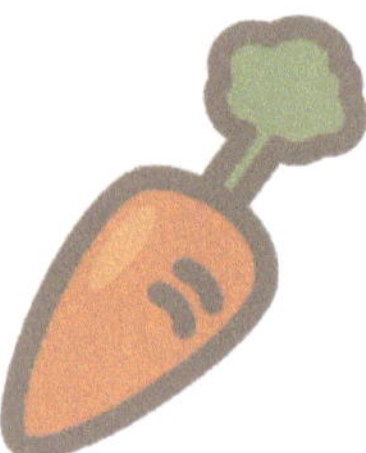 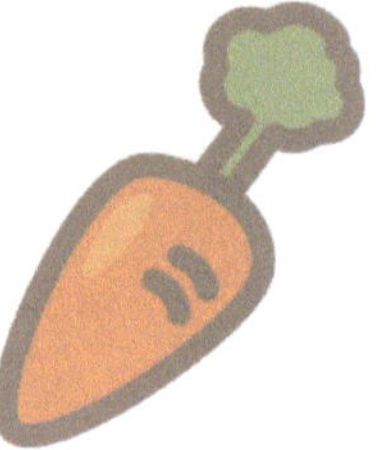

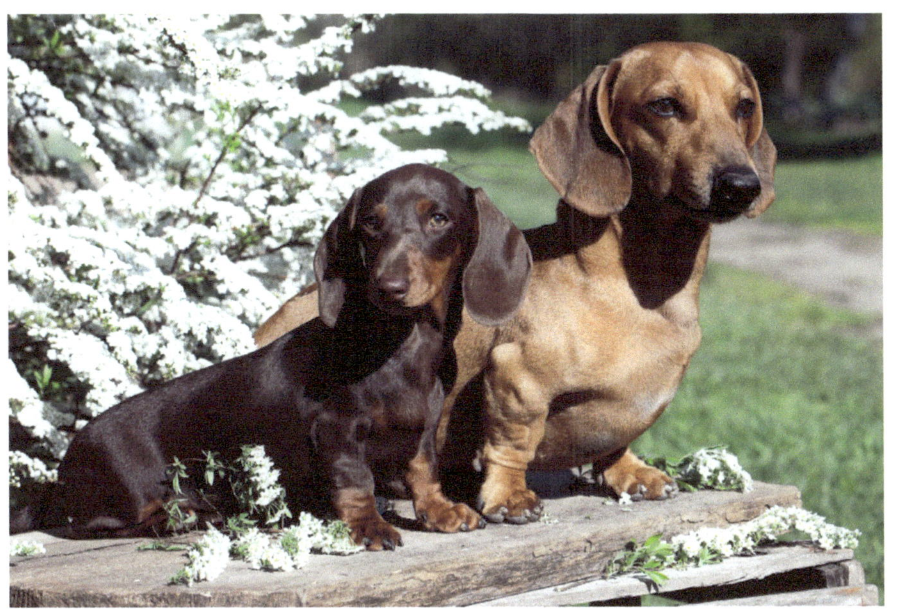

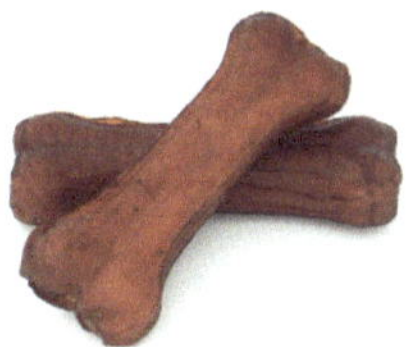 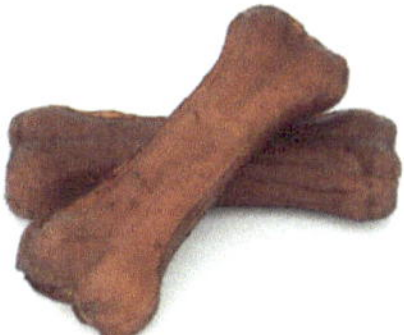 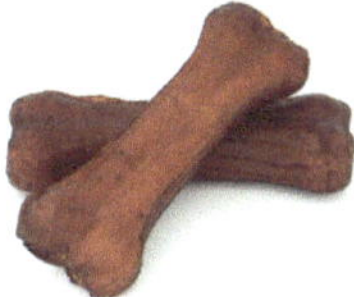

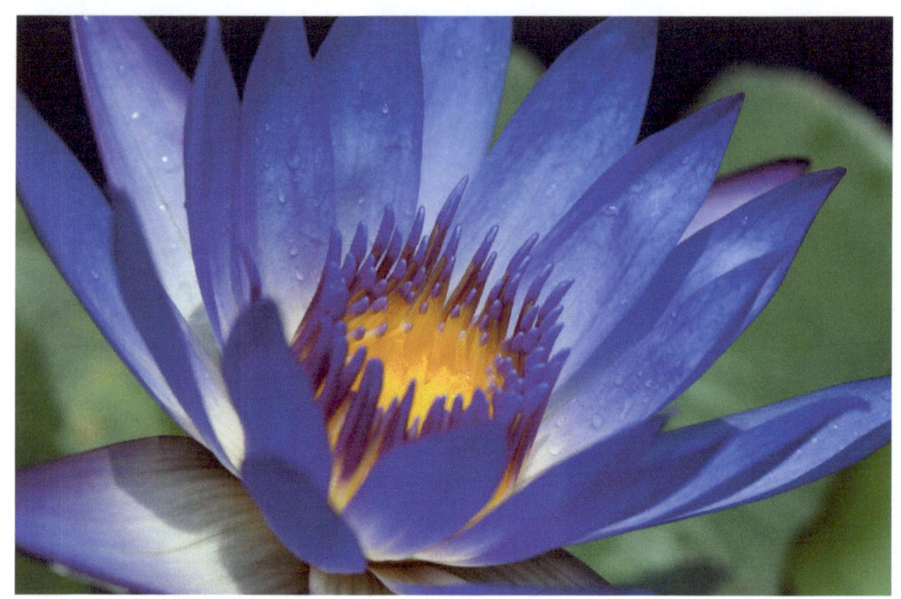

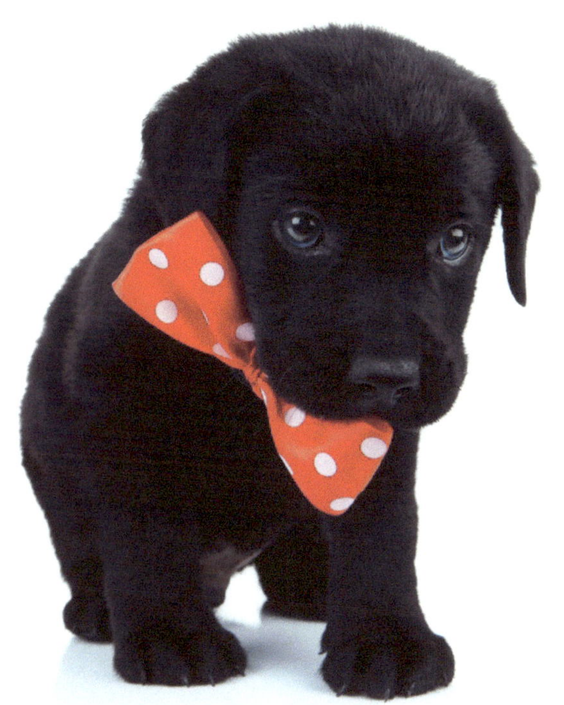

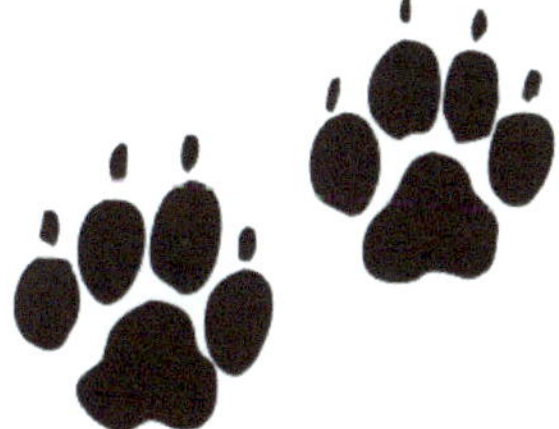 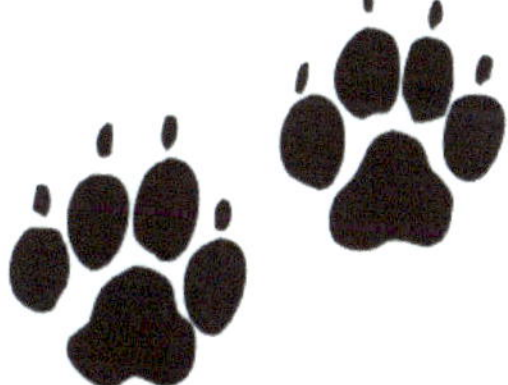

Learning is fun

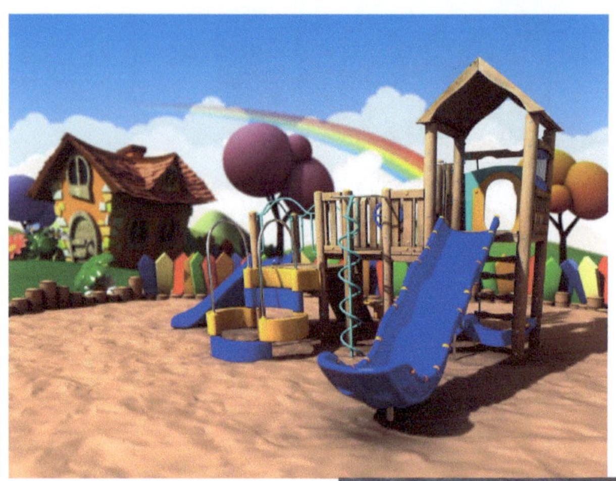

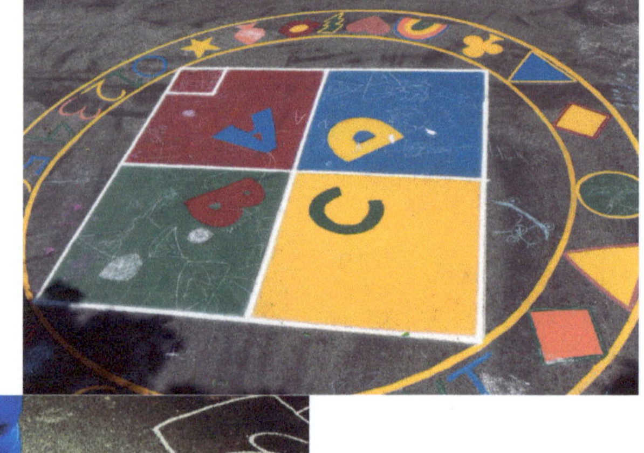

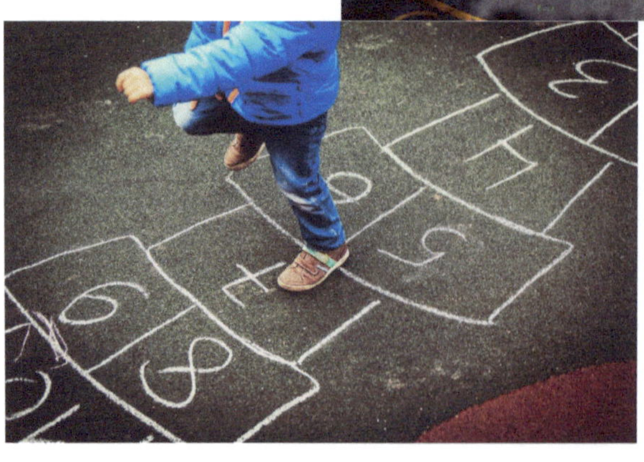